PageMaker 7: Advanced

Student Manual

THOMSON

COURSE TECHNOLOGY

Australia • Canada • Mexico • Singapore
Spain • United Kingdom • United States

PageMaker 7: Advanced

VP and GM of Courseware:	Michael Springer
Series Product Managers:	Caryl Bahner-Guhin and Adam A. Wilcox
Developmental Editor:	Jim O'Shea
Copyeditor:	Cathy Albano
Keytester:	Cliff Coryea
Series Designer:	Adam A. Wilcox
Cover Designer:	Steve Deschene

For more information contact:

Course Technology
25 Thomson Place
Boston, MA 02210

Or find us on the Web at: www.course.com

For permission to use material from this text or product, submit a request online at: www.thomsonrights.com

Any additional questions about permissions can be submitted by e-mail to: thomsonrights@thomson.com

ISBN 0-619-20475-3

Printed in the United States of America

2 3 4 5 PM 06 05 04

Contents

PageMaker 7: Advanced

Introduction

After reading this introduction, you will know how to:

A Use Course Technology ILT manuals in general.

B Use prerequisites, a target student description, course objectives, and a skills inventory to properly set your expectations for the course.

C Re-key this course after class.

Topic A: About the manual

Course Technology ILT philosophy

Course Technology ILT manuals facilitate your learning by providing structured interaction with the software itself. While we provide text to explain difficult concepts, the hands-on activities are the focus of our courses. By paying close attention as your instructor leads you through these activities, you will learn the skills and concepts effectively.

We believe strongly in the instructor-led classroom. During class, focus on your instructor. Our manuals are designed and written to facilitate your interaction with your instructor, and not to call attention to the manuals themselves.

We believe in the basic approach of setting expectations, delivering instruction, and providing summary and review afterwards. For this reason, lessons begin with objectives and end with summaries. We also provide overall course objectives and a course summary to provide both an introduction to and closure on the entire course.

Manual components

The manuals contain these major components:

- Table of contents
- Introduction
- Units
- Course summary
- Quick reference
- Index

Each element is described below.

Table of contents

The table of contents acts as a learning roadmap.

Introduction

The introduction contains information about our training philosophy and our manual components, features, and conventions. It contains target student, prerequisite, objective, and setup information for the specific course.

Units

Units are the largest structural component of the course content. A unit begins with a title page that lists objectives for each major subdivision, or topic, within the unit. Within each topic, conceptual and explanatory information alternates with hands-on activities. Units conclude with a summary comprising one paragraph for each topic, and an independent practice activity that gives you an opportunity to practice the skills you've learned.

The conceptual information takes the form of text paragraphs, exhibits, lists, and tables. The activities are structured in two columns, one telling you what to do, the other providing explanations, descriptions, and graphics.

Course summary

This section provides a text summary of the entire course. It is useful for providing closure at the end of the course. The course summary also indicates the next course in this series, if there is one, and lists additional resources you might find useful as you continue to learn about the software.

Quick reference

The quick reference is an at-a-glance job aid summarizing some of the more common features of the software.

Index

The index enables you to quickly find information about a particular feature or concept of the software.

Manual conventions

We've tried to keep the number of elements and the types of formatting to a minimum in the manuals. This aids in clarity and makes the manuals more classically elegant looking. But there are some conventions and icons you should know about.

Convention/icon	Description
Italic text	In conceptual text, indicates a new term or feature.
Bold text	In unit summaries, indicates a key term or concept. In an independent practice activity, indicates an explicit item that you select, choose, or type.
`Code font`	Indicates code or syntax.
Select **bold item**	In the left column of hands-on activities, bold sans-serif text indicates an explicit item that you select, choose, or type.
Keycaps like ↵ ENTER	Indicate a key on the keyboard you must press.

Hands-on activities

The hands-on activities are the most important parts of our manuals. They are divided into two primary columns. The "Here's how" column gives short instructions to you about what to do. The "Here's why" column provides explanations, graphics, and clarifications. Here's a sample:

Do it!

A-1:   Creating a commission formula

Here's how	Here's why
1 Open Sales	This is an oversimplified sales compensation worksheet. It shows sales totals, commissions, and incentives for five sales reps.
2 Observe the contents of cell F4	F4 ▼ = =E4*C_Rate
	The commission rate formulas use the name "C_Rate" instead of a value for the commission rate.

For these activities, we have provided a collection of data files designed to help you learn each skill in a real-world business context. As you work through the activities, you will modify and update these files. Of course, you might make a mistake and, therefore, want to re-key the activity starting from scratch. To make it easy to start over, you will rename each data file at the end of the first activity in which the file is modified. Our convention for renaming files is to add the word "My" to the beginning of the file name. In the above activity, for example, a file called "Sales" is being used for the first time. At the end of this activity, you would save the file as "My sales," thus leaving the "Sales" file unchanged. If you make a mistake, you can start over using the original "Sales" file.

In some activities, however, it may not be practical to rename the data file. If you want to retry one of these activities, ask your instructor for a fresh copy of the original data file.

Topic B: Setting your expectations

Properly setting your expectations is essential to your success. This topic will help you do that by providing:

- Prerequisites for this course
- A description of the target student at whom the course is aimed
- A list of the objectives for the course
- A skills assessment for the course

Course prerequisites

Before taking this course, you should be familiar with personal computers and the use of a keyboard and a mouse. Furthermore, this course assumes that you've completed the following courses or have equivalent experience:

- *PageMaker 7.0: Intermediate*

Target student

You should have knowledge of Adobe PageMaker 7.0. You will get the most out of this course if your goal is to become proficient in using PageMaker 7.0's advanced features for applying colors, publishing publications, and printing publications.

Course objectives

These overall course objectives will give you an idea about what to expect from the course. It is also possible that they will help you see that this course is not the right one for you. If you think you either lack the prerequisite knowledge or already know most of the subject matter to be covered, you should let your instructor know that you think you are misplaced in the class.

After completing this course, you will know how to:

- Use the story editor to check spelling, find and replace text, delete extra spaces and returns, change text attributes, use typography techniques to adjust line length, select a typeface, and use hyphenation and justification.

- Use the Colors palette to select a color model; create and use a spot, process, and tint color; convert one color type to another; add a color from a color library; apply colors to multiple objects and imported objects; and create a custom color library.

- Set up and change the preferences of a Color Management System, select image profiles, and set and use trapping techniques.

- Use scripts to automate PageMaker processes and use plug-ins to create and perform advanced PageMaker processes.

- Import an HTML file to PageMaker, create a PDF document, set the PDF options, create a hyperlink, convert a publication to an HTML document, and use the Layout Adjustment option to adjust page elements.

- Perform prepress processes by using Image Control; create a PostScript file; create, modify, and use printer styles; understand screen and printer fonts; and print color separations.

Skills inventory

Use the following form to gauge your skill level entering the class. For each skill listed, rate your familiarity from 1 to 5, with 5 being the most familiar. *This is not a test.* Rather, it is intended to provide you with an idea of where you're starting from at the beginning of class. If you're wholly unfamiliar with all the skills, you might not be ready for the class. If you think you already understand all of the skills, you might need to move on to the next course in the series. In either case, you should let your instructor know as soon as possible.

Skill	1	2	3	4	5
Checking the spelling					
Finding and Replacing text					
Changing text attributes					
Adjusting line length and using hyphenation and justification					
Changing the color model					
Creating and using a spot, process, and tint color					
Converting a spot color to a process color					
Selecting a color from a color library					
Creating a custom color library					
Applying colors to multiple objects					
Applying colors to imported objects					
Setting CMS preferences					
Creating an image profile					
Using the Trapping Preferences dialog box					
Using the Scripts palette and running a script					
Using a plug-in					
Importing an HTML file to PageMaker					
Creating a PDF document					
Adding hyperlinks to publications					

Skill	**1**	**2**	**3**	**4**	**5**
Using the automatic Layout Adjustment option					
Exporting a publication to HTML format					
Using Image Control					
Creating a PostScript file					
Creating, modifying, and using a printer style					
Printing color separations					

Topic C: Re-keying the course

If you have the proper hardware and software, you can re-key this course after class. This section explains what you'll need in order to do so, and how to do it.

Computer requirements

To re-key this course, your personal computer must have:

- A keyboard and a mouse
- An Intel Pentium II or higher (Intel Pentium III or higher preferred)
- 128 MB RAM
- At least 320 MB of available hard drive space (for the software and data files)
- A CD-ROM drive
- An SVGA monitor (800×600 minimum resolution support)
- An Adobe PostScript driver (A printer is not required.)
- A typical setup of Windows 2000 Professional Edition installed according to the software manufacturer's instructions.
- Adobe PageMaker 7.0 installed according to the software manufacturer's instructions.
- Internet access is required if you will be downloading data files from www.courseilt.com/instructor_tools.htm.

Setup instructions to re-key the course

Before you re-key the course, you will need to perform the following steps.

1   Install Microsoft Windows 2000 Professional according to the software manufacturer's instructions. Install the latest critical updates and service packs from www.windowsupdate.com on your computer. You can also use Windows XP Professional, although the screen shots in this course were taken using Windows 2000 Professional, and your screens might look somewhat different.

2   Set the screen resolution to 800×600, and set the screen colors to True Color (24 bit or 32 bit). If you use a different resolution, the page magnification settings in each activity will be off, and the screen captures in this manual might not match what students see on their monitors.

3   Install Adobe PageMaker 7.0 according to the software manufacturer's instructions.

    a   In the Language Selection dialog box, verify that U.S. English is selected.

    b   Perform a Typical installation with all the default options.

4   Perform a Typical installation of Acrobat Distiller 5 and Acrobat Reader 5.

5   Install the Adobe PostScript driver from the PageMaker CD as a local printer with the default options:

   a   From the Available ports list, select LPT1.

   b   In the Printers list, select Generic PostScript Driver.

   c   Set this printer as the default printer. (The target printer of all the data files for this course is set as this driver. If you don't install this specific driver, when the you open the files, they will get an error message indicating that the target printer is missing. However, you can still open the file by clicking Continue.)

6   Close the Adobe Registration dialog box:

   a   Open PageMaker and the Adobe Registration dialog box will appear.

   b   Select Do not display this dialog again.

   c   Click Continue.

7   Change the application preferences. Here's how:

   a   Choose File, Preferences, General to open the Preferences dialog box.

   b   Change the Measurements in list to Picas, and change the Vertical rule list to Picas.

   c   Under the Graphics display option, select High resolution.

   d   Click OK.

   e   Close PageMaker.

8   Download the Student Data examples for the course. (If you do not have an Internet connection, you can ask your instructor for a copy of the data files on a diskette.)

   a   Connect to www.courseilt.com/instructor_tools.html.

   b   Click the link for Adobe PageMaker to display a page of course listings, and then click the link for PageMaker 7.0: Advanced.

   c   Click the link for downloading the data disk files, and follow the instructions that appear on your screen.

9   Copy the data files for the course to the Student Data folder.

Unit 1

Proofing publications

Unit time: 75 minutes

Complete this unit, and you'll know how to:

A Use the story editor to check spelling, find and replace text, delete extra spaces and returns, and change text attributes.

B Adjust line length, select a typeface, and use hyphenation and justification.

Topic A: Working with the story editor

Explanation

When you create a publication in PageMaker, it is important that you proofread the text before the final output. This task is much easier when you use PageMaker's story editor. By using the story editor, you can check the spelling, change text attributes, find text, and replace text.

Story editor

The *story editor* is PageMaker's built-in word processor, which you use to type and proof text. After you open the story editor, you can work with text regardless of its placement in the page layout. This helps to easily check spelling, change text attributes, and find and replace text without having to wait for the layout and large graphic images to be refreshed.

To open the story editor, select a block of text and choose Edit, Edit Story. You can also click the text three times with the Pointer tool to open the story editor.

Spelling dialog box

Once the story editor is open, you can use the Spelling dialog box to check for misspelled words and to correct them. You cannot perform a spelling check in Page Layout view. The various options for checking spelling are listed in the following table.

Options	Description
Alternate spellings	Displays alternate correct words for a misspelled word.
Show duplicates	Displays repeated words that appear next to each other.
Search document	Checks the spelling for the Current publication or All publications.
Search story	Checks the spelling within the Selected text, Current story, or All stories.
Ignore	Ignores the misspelled word.
Replace	Replaces the misspelled word.
Add	Adds a word to the PageMaker dictionary.

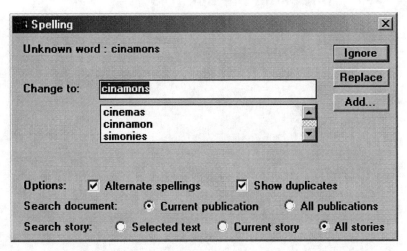

Exhibit 1-1: The Spelling dialog box with cinamons *selected as a misspelled word*

Do it!

A-1: Checking the spelling

Here's how	Here's why
1 Start Adobe PageMaker 7.0	Choose Start, Programs, Adobe, PageMaker 7.0, Adobe PageMaker 7.0.
2 Close the Templates palette	If necessary.
Close the Picture palette	If necessary.
3 Open Proofing	From the current unit folder.
4 Save the publication as **My proofing**	In the current unit folder.
5 Switch to Actual Size view	
Click the Method text block three times	To open the story editor.
Observe the window	Only the text elements appear in the window.
6 Choose **Utilities, Spelling...**	To open the Spelling dialog box.
7 Next to Search document, observe that Current publication is selected	You'll check the spelling in the current publication. You can also check spelling in other publications by selecting All publications.
Next to Search story, select **All stories**	You are going to perform a spelling check on all stories in the publication. All the stories will open in the story editor, but only one story will be visible on screen at a time.
8 Click **Start**	To start the spelling check. The first misspelled word, "cinamons," appears at the top of the dialog box, as shown in Exhibit 1-1.
9 Observe the Change to box	The misspelled word appears in this box.
Observe the list	It displays alternate words.
10 From the list, select **cinnamon**	You'll replace "cinamons" with "cinnamon." Now, the Change to box displays "cinnamon."
Click **Replace**	To replace the misspelled word with "cinnamon." Now, the next misspelled word. "litle," appears at the top of the dialog box and in the Change to box.
Replace the word with **little**	(From the list, select little and click Replace.) The next misspelled word "tbsp" appears.

11 Click **Add**	**Add Word to User Dictionary** [x] Word: [tb~~~sp] OK Dictionary: [US English ▼] Cancel Add: ○ As all lowercase ⊙ Exactly as typed Remove To add "tbsp" into the PageMaker dictionary. The Add Word to User Dictionary dialog box appears.
12 Observe the Word box	The word appears with tildes (~). The tildes indicate the discretionary hyphen for the word. Discretionary hyphens indicate the suggested location for breaking a word if it appears at the end of a line. Removing a discretionary hyphen will ensure that the word is moved to a new line instead of breaking it up at the end of a line.
Click **OK**	To close the dialog box.
13 Click **Continue**	The next misspelled word, "tsp," appears.
14 Click **Ignore**	To ignore the suggestion. The next misspelled word, "tbls," appears.
Ignore the word "tbls"	Click Ignore.
15 Observe the dialog box	**Spelling** **Spelling check complete.** A message appears indicating that the spelling check is complete.
16 Close the dialog box	The story editor is still open.
17 Update the publication	

Find and replace text

Explanation

When you proof publications, you might want to swap a specific word with another word. To do that, use the Change dialog box to search a text block or a publication for a specific word and replace it with another. You can also use the Find dialog box to find text, but you cannot use it to replace text.

To find and replace text:

1 Open the story editor.

2 Choose Utilities, Change to open the Change dialog box.

3 In the Find what box, enter the text you want to find.

4 In the Change to box, enter new text.

5 Click Find.

6 Click Change to replace the highlighted occurrence or Change all to replace all occurrences of the text.

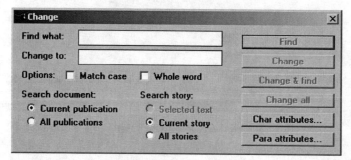

Exhibit 1-2: The Change dialog box

To use the find text feature without replacing any text, open the story editor. Choose Utilities, Find to open the Find dialog box. In the Find what box, enter the text you are looking for and click Find.

Do it!   **A-2:   Finding and replacing text**

Here's how	Here's why
1 Choose **Utilities, Change...**	To open the Change dialog box, as shown in Exhibit 1-2.
2 In the Find what box, enter **OS**	You'll search for this word.
3 In the Change to box, enter **Outlander Spices**	You'll change the abbreviation "OS" to "Outlander Spices."
4 Next to Options, check **Match case**	You'll search only for words that match the case of the text you entered in the Find what box.
Next to Options, check **Whole word**	You'll search only for words that match the Find what criteria exactly.
Under Search story, select **All stories**	You'll search all the stories in the publication.
5 Click **Find**	To find the word. PageMaker selects the first occurrence of "OS."
Click **Change**	To change the word to "Outlander Spices."
6 Click **Find next**	To find the next occurrence of "OS."
Click **Change & find**	To change the word to "Outlander Spices" and find the next occurrence of "OS."
7 Click **Change all**	To replace all the occurrences of "OS" with "Outlander Spices."
8 Close the dialog box	
Deselect the text	
9 Update the publication	

Extra characters

Explanation

When using a typewriter, each character has an equal width, and as a result, it is common practice to type two spaces after a sentence or a colon. In Windows applications, characters have proportional widths and consequently need only one space after sentences and colons.

Because of this, many people who learned how to type on a typewriter will often add two spaces after a sentence or colon out of habit. To remove these extra spaces in a story:

1 Open the Change dialog box.
2 In the Find what box, press the Spacebar two times.
3 In the Change to box, press the Spacebar.
4 Click Find.
5 Click Change all.

The story editor uses paragraph symbols to represent spaces, returns, and tabs. You choose Story, Display ¶ to view the paragraph symbols. Once the symbols are displayed, you will notice that a dot (.) represents a space, a ¶ for a return, and an arrow for a tab.

Extra returns

When you add new paragraphs, it is common to press Enter twice to add space between the paragraphs. These extra returns create unnecessary blank lines in a publication. You can easily remove the extra returns in a story by using the Change dialog box. To do so:

1 Open the Change dialog box.
2 In the Find what box, enter ^p^p. (In the story editor, ^p represents a return.)
3 In the Change to box, enter ^p.
4 Click Find.
5 Click Change all.

Do it!

A-3: Deleting extra spaces and returns

Here's how	Here's why
1 Choose **Story, Display ¶**	To display the paragraph symbols. The story editor shows a dot (.) for a space, ¶ for a return, and an arrow for a tab.
2 Open the Change dialog box	Choose Utilities, Change.
3 Verify the text in the Find what box is selected	
Press (SPACEBAR) two times	Typing replaces the selection. You'll find extra spaces in the story.
4 Select the text in the Change to box	Press Tab and the text in the Change to box will be selected.
Press (SPACEBAR)	You'll change double spaces to single spaces.

5 Next to Options, clear
   Match case

   Next to Options, clear
   Whole word

6 Under Search document, verify
   that Current publication is
   selected

You'll remove extra spaces in the current
document.

   Under Search story, select
   All stories

You'll find and remove extra spaces in all the
stories.

7 Click **Find**

To find the first occurrence of the extra space.

   Click **Change all**

(If a message box appears, prompting you to
continue from the beginning of a story, click
Yes.) To replace all double spaces with single
spaces.

8 Edit the Find what box to read
   ^p^p

Remove the double space you entered in this
box before editing it. You'll search for extra
returns. PageMaker uses ^p to recognize a
return.

   Edit the Change to box to read **^p**

Remove the single space you entered in this box
before editing it. You'll replace double returns
with a single return.

9 Click **Change all**

(If a message box appears, prompting you to
continue from the beginning of story, click Yes.)
To remove all extra returns.

10 Close the dialog box

11 Close the story

Click the Close button.

12 Close all open stories

To return to the publication.

13 Update the publication

Text attributes

Explanation   Another use of the Change dialog box is to search for specific text and replace the formatting of that text with other attributes. To do so:

1   Open the story editor.

2   Open the Change dialog box.

3   In the Find what box, enter the text. You will search for and change the attributes of this text.

4   In the Change to box, enter the same text you entered in the Find what box. This will ensure that only the text attributes are changed.

5   In the Change dialog box, click Char attributes to open the Change Character Attributes dialog box, as shown in Exhibit 1-3.

6   From the Find what section, select the attributes you want to search for or leave the attributes set to "any."

7   From the Change to section, select the new attributes to apply to the text.

8   Click OK to close the Change Character Attributes dialog box.

9   Click Find in Change dialog box to find text.

10 Click Change to replace the highlighted occurrence or Change all to replace all occurrences of the indicated text attributes.

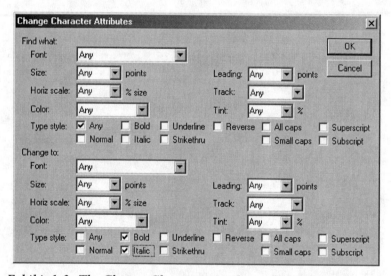

Exhibit 1-3: The Change Character Attributes dialog box

Do it!   **A-4:   Changing text attributes**

Here's how	Here's why
1 Move to the second page	
2 Triple-click the text below the heading	To open the story editor.
Place the insertion point at the beginning of the text	If necessary.
3 Open the Change dialog box	Choose Utilities, Change.
4 Edit the Find what box to read **Outlander Spices**	You'll change the attributes of this text.
5 Edit the Change to box to read **Outlander Spices**	You'll keep the same text and just edit the attributes.
6 Click **Char attributes**	To open the Change Character Attributes dialog box.
In the Find what section, observe the options	All of the options have Any selected. You'll search for occurrences of "Outlander Spices" that have any attributes applied.
In the Change to section, next to Type style, check **Bold**	You'll apply the Bold type style to occurrences of "Outlander Spices."
In the Change to section, next to Type style, check **Italic**	You'll apply the Italic type style to occurrences of "Outlander Spices."
7 Click **OK**	To close the dialog box and return to the Change dialog box.
8 Click **Find**	To find the first occurrence of the text "Outlander Spices."
Click **Change**	To apply the specified attributes to the text.
9 Apply the attributes to the next instance of the text	
10 Close the dialog box	
11 Close the story editor	
12 Update and close the publication	

Topic B: Using typography techniques

Explanation
When creating a publication, you have to follow certain typographical techniques to get a professional output. These techniques improve the readability of text and also the appearance of the entire layout design. They include adjusting line length, selecting the correct typeface, and using hyphenation and justification.

Typefaces

The layout of a publication is important because it determines how it communicates ideas and content to readers. Just as important are the typefaces applied to the text.

A *typeface* is the font or letter design, and can be broken into two categories, serif and sans serif.

Both of these categories contain different designs. For example, Times New Roman is a commonly used serif font and Arial is a sans serif font.

To apply and modify the typefaces, you select the text and use the Styles palette or the Control palette. The following table further describes the two typefaces.

Typeface	Example	Description
Serif	Outlander Spices (Garamond)	This typeface has cross strokes at the end of each character's main stroke. It is normally used with body text. Examples include Garamond and Times New Roman
Sans serif	Outlander Spices (Arial)	This typeface does not have cross strokes at the end-of-character main strokes. It is normally used with headings and captions. Examples: Verdana and Arial

Text elements

When designing a publication, you need to arrange text so that it will retain the reader's interest and be easy to read. The text is usually arranged as elements on a page and is generally divided into three categories: headings, captions, and body text. Each is designed to present information in the best possible format.

Headings and captions are short in length and are often used to present small amounts of information. For example, a newsletter might have a headline of "Fourth Quarter Profits Are Up" and a caption under a photograph that says, "This is the new product line that has propelled fourth quarter profits." Because these lines are short and need to stand out, it is a good idea to use a sans serif typeface for both, but a small font size for the caption and a large one for the headline.

The body text normally contains many paragraphs of information. This means it will require an effort to read and so the typeface needs to make that task as easy as possible. With that in mind, it is best to use a serif typeface with a small-to-medium font size. This will ensure that it is not difficult for the reader to spent time reading the entire body of text.

Do it! **B-1: Discussing a typeface**

Questions and answers

1 You are creating a newsletter using PageMaker. You decide to use the Verdana and Times New Roman fonts in this publication. Which font should you use for the body text? Why?

2 You decide to use Verdana for headings and subheadings. After applying the font, you realize that the main headings and subheadings look too much alike. How can you solve this problem?

Line length

When you place a large amount of text in a single column that is the width of the page, the lines of text will be long and difficult to read, and will decrease the reader's interest. Consequently, it is a good typographical practice to keep the number of characters per line to less than 50. To do this, you can divide a page into multiple columns and place the text in those columns. Meaning, you will be breaking the paragraphs into smaller, more manageable chunks.

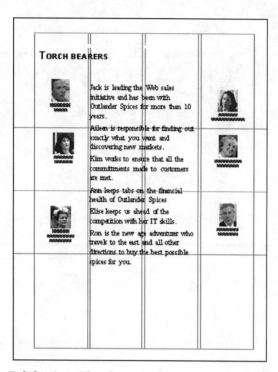

Exhibit 1-4: The elements of a page arranged in multiple columns

Do it!

B-2:   Adjusting the line length

Here's how	Here's why
1 Open Typography	From the current unit folder.
Maximize the window	If necessary.
2 Save the publication as **My typography**	
3 Observe the page	The text flows in a single column from the left margin to the right margin.
4 Open the Column Guides dialog box	Choose Layout, Column Guides.
In the Number of columns box, enter **4**	You'll add four columns in the page.
In the Space between columns box, enter **0p6**	To specify the space between columns as six points. To specify the space between columns as six points.
Click **OK**	
	To close the dialog box and add four columns.
5 Select the text block under the heading	You'll arrange the line length of this text block.
6 Resize the upper-left corner handle of the text block, as shown	
	To reduce the width of the text block. The text is then moved down and extends beyond the bottom of the text block. As a result, the bottom windowshade handle becomes red.

7 Resize the width of the text block, as shown

> TORCH BEARERS
>
> Jack is leading the Web sales initiative and has been with Outlander Spices for more than 10 years.
>
> Aileen is responsible for finding out exactly what you want and discovering new markets.
>
> Kim works to ensure that all the committments made to customers are met.
>
> Ann keeps tabs on the financial

8 Move the photos and captions to the Pasteboard

Select a photo and the corresponding caption. Then, move the selections to the pasteboard. Repeat for each photo and caption.

9 Drag the bottom windowshade handle down

To increase the height to fit the entire text within the text block.

10 Draw horizontal ruler guides at 21p, 33p, and 45p

(Point the mouse pointer to the horizontal ruler and drag it to the required location in the vertical ruler.) Use the Control palette to place the ruler guides at the correct locations.

11 Arrange the photos, captions, and the heading

As shown in Exhibit 1-4.

12 Update the publication

Hyphenation and justification

Explanation
When you justify text, PageMaker aligns it to both the left and right sides of the text block. If the text is not hyphenated, long words will go to the next line. This might create wide gaps between words in a line. If you hyphenate words in a paragraph, the long words break with a hyphen at the end of the line and continue on the next line, as shown in Exhibit 1-5.

To apply hyphenation, select the text and choose Type, Hyphenation to display the Hyphenation dialog box, as shown in Exhibit 1-6. Make the necessary changes in the dialog box and click OK.

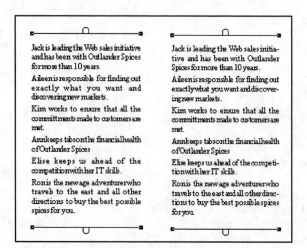

Exhibit 1-5: A sample text with and without hyphenation

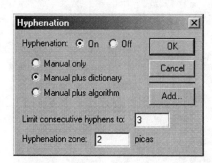

Exhibit 1-6: The Hyphenation dialog box

B-3:   Using hyphenation and justification

Here's how	Here's why
1 Select the text in the second and third columns	(Use the Text tool.) You'll change this text's alignment.
2 Click the Paragraph-view button	In the Control palette.
Click ▤	(If necessary.) The justify button is in the Control palette. To justify the text.
Observe the text	Now the text is justified. The words are not hyphenated and there are long gaps between some words.
3 Choose **Type**, **Hyphenation…**	To open the Hyphenation dialog box.
4 Next to Hyphenation, select **On**	You'll add hyphenation to words.
5 Edit the Limit consecutive hyphens to box to read **3**	To limit the number of consecutive hyphens. You set this option to avoid repeat hyphens in a paragraph.
Edit the Hyphenation zone box to read **2**	To set the space between the right margin guide or column guide and the hyphenated word.
Click **OK**	To close the Hyphenation dialog box and apply the changes.
6 Deselect the text	
Observe the text	Now the words "initiative," "discovering," "competition," and "directions" are hyphenated.
7 Update and close the publication	

Unit summary: Proofing publications

Topic A   In this topic, you learned how to use the **story editor** to **check the spelling**, **find** and **replace** text, **remove** extra spaces and returns, and **change text attributes** of a publication.

Topic B   In this topic, you learned how to **adjust line length**, select a **typeface**, and apply **hyphenation** and **justification** to a publication.

Independent practice activity

1 Open Proofing practice.

2 Save the publication as **My proofing practice**.

3 Open the story editor and check the spelling in all the stories.

4 Remove extra spaces and extra returns in all the stories.

5 Find the word "**soup**" in all the stories and replace it with "**soups**."
   (Hint: Remove the Char attributes before replacing the text.)

6 Close the story editor.

7 Add **four** columns with a **0p6** space between the columns.

8 Draw horizontal ruler guides at **18p**, **36p**, and **54p**.

9 Arrange the text blocks and pictures, as shown in Exhibit 1-7.

10 Justify the text in the **Cinnamon**, **Nutmeg**, **Bay leaf**, and **Clove** text blocks.

11 Add hyphenation to the text blocks. (Hint: Enter **2** in both Limit consecutive hyphens to and Hyphenation zone boxes.)

12 Update and close the publication.

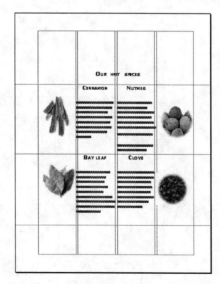

Exhibit 1-7: The page layout after step 9 of the Independent Practice Activity

Unit 2
Working with colors

Unit time: 65 minutes

Complete this unit, and you'll know how to:

A Select a color model; create and use a spot, process, and tint color; and convert one color type to another.

B Add a color to the Colors palette from a color library and create a custom color library.

C Use the Colors palette to apply colors to multiple objects and imported objects.

Topic A: Using colors

Explanation

In PageMaker, you can use the colors available in the Colors palette to enhance the look and feel of images and graphics in a publication. To do this, you select an object or text and then use the Colors palette to either apply or remove specific colors. In addition, you can also use the Colors palette to create your own colors, import them from existing publications, or import colors from other images.

When you create a color you need to choose the color model and the type of color. There are three color models (RGB, HLS, and CMYK) and three types of colors (spot, process, and tint).

The Colors palette

By default, the black, blue, cyan, green, magenta, red, and yellow colors are available in the Colors palette. If you need a different color, click the New color button to open the Color Options dialog box. To modify an existing color, double-click the color in the Colors palette and modify it in the Color Options dialog box. To remove a color from the palette, select a color and click the Trash button.

In the Colors palette, along with a color, you can see two icons that represent the color model and the color type, as shown in Exhibit 2-1.

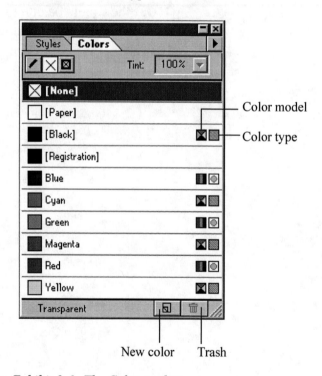

Exhibit 2-1: The Colors palette

Color model

Color models are a range of colors that can be viewed on your monitor or printed. PageMaker supports three color models. The following table describes the different models.

Model	Icon	Description
RGB	▮	Based on the three primary colors of the visible light spectrum: red, green, and blue. By mixing these three basic components of colored light in various proportions and intensities, a large percentage of the visible spectrum can be represented. You can create secondary colors by mixing the primary colors in different proportions and intensities. Primary colors are also called additive colors because they are combined to produce white. The additive colors are used for lighting, film recorders, video, and monitors.
CMYK	▨	Based on four colors: cyan, magenta, yellow, and black. This model is based on the light-absorbing quality of ink printed on paper. According to the color theory, cyan, magenta, and yellow are combined to absorb all color and produce black. Hence, the colors in the CMYK model are also called subtractive colors. These colors are used for printing.
HLS	▦	Resembles colors used by painters. Stands for Hue, Lightness, and Saturation. Hue refers to the position of the color in the visible color spectrum. Lightness is the amount of light reflected by the color. Saturation is the color intensity. This color model gives a close approximation to traditional colors used by artists and painters.

Do it!

A-1: Changing the color model

Here's how	Here's why
1 Observe the color model icon for the color blue	▮ Blue ▮ ▣
	This icon represents the RGB color model.
2 In the Colors palette, double-click **Blue**	(The Color Options dialog box appears.) You'll change the color model of this color.
Observe the Model box	The current color model is RGB. RGB colors are used for electronic display.
3 From the Model list, select **CMYK**	CMYK colors are printable inks.
4 Click **OK**	Blue ▨ ▣
	To close the dialog box. The color model icon changes.

Color types

Explanation

PageMaker has three color types, which are explained in the following table.

Type	Icon	Description
Spot	◎	A solid color prepared by using only one ink
Process	▩	Prepared by mixing the four inks of the CMYK model
Tint	A % sign appears preceding the color model and color type icons	Prepared by varying the intensity of a spot color

Spot color

You use a spot color when you have one, two, or three colors in a publication. If you have four or more colors, it makes more sense to use process color. As a general rule, using spot color will lower your publishing costs.

Do it!   **A-2:   Creating and using a spot color**

Here's how	Here's why
1 Open Colors	From the current unit folder.
Maximize the window	If necessary.
2 Save the publication as **My colors**	In the current unit folder.
3 Click [🔲]	(The New color button is in the Colors palette.) To open the Color Options dialog box.
4 In the Name box, enter **My red**	You'll create a red color.
5 Observe the Type box	The color type is Spot.
6 Edit the Red box to read **200**	
Edit the Green box to read **55**	
Edit the Blue box to read **55**	
Press (TAB)	You'll see a dark shade of red in the upper part of the preview area.
7 Click **OK**	(To close the Color Options dialog box.) The new color My red appears in the Colors palette.
8 Observe the color type icon	The icon shows a filled circle inside a square, indicating that it is a spot color.
9 Select the orange bar to the left of the cover page	You'll change the color to My red.
Change the Line and Fill color to My red	
10 Update the publication	

Process color

Explanation

Most publications that are professionally printed are done so by using process colors. They are more expensive than spot colors but give you additional flexibility and access to an almost a limitless number of color combinations.

A *process color* refers to a color that is created by mixing three or four inks. These are primary inks and are used to create different colors and shades by mixing them in varying proportions. For example, the CMYK colors are created by mixing four inks, cyan, magenta, yellow, and black. With these four inks, it is possible to create an extremely wide range of colors.

In PageMaker, you can also create RGB and HLS process colors. However, when the document is printed, these colors will be mapped to the nearest CMYK color. This is because most printing processes use the CMYK model for printing color publications.

You can create a process color by choosing Process from the Type list in the Color Options dialog box. You can then mix the four inks by using the color sliders to get the color you want.

Do it!

A-3:   Creating a process color

Here's how	Here's why
1 Click ▣	To open the Color Options dialog box.
2 In the Name box, enter **My blue**	
3 From the Type list, select **Process**	
4 From the Model list, select **CMYK**	To create a CMYK process color.
5 Edit the Cyan, Magenta, Yellow, and Black boxes to read **65**, **50**, **30**, and **20,** respectively	You'll save this color as a process color.
6 Click **OK**	(To close the Color Options dialog box.) The shade My blue appears in the Colors palette.
Observe the color type icon	▣ My blue ☒▣
	The icon is a filled square indicating that it is a process color.
7 Update the publication	

Tint color

Explanation

If you want to keep printing costs low, use a spot color and create shades of the same color. These shades will be created from the same ink. For example, you can create shades of blue by specifying the percentage of the ink to be used. You can create tints as separate colors in the palette or change the percentage of a color from the Tint list in the Colors palette.

Do it!

A-4:   Creating a tint color

Here's how	Here's why
1 Open the Color Options dialog box	Click the new color button in the Colors palette.
2 In the Name box, enter **My red tint**	
3 From the Type list, select **Tint**	
4 From the Base Color list, select **My red**	If necessary.
5 Edit the Tint box to read **50**	To change the intensity of the color.
6 Click **OK**	The My red tint color appears in the Colors palette.
Observe the color My red tint	My red tint % ▮ ◉
	A percentage sign appears to the left of the color model and color type icons.
7 Select the text **Outlander**	Click the Text tool before selecting.
8 Change the text color to My red tint	
Deselect the text	The color of the text is a tint of the color My red.
9 Update the publication	

Convert spot colors to process color

Explanation

In the professional printing process, each color or ink that is used will have its own printing plate. Printing plates are templates that contain the contents, including graphics, to be printed. The colors are mixed and transferred through these printing plates. A printing press, by default, will use the four printing plates of the CMYK model, which gives a choice of using a wide variety of colors.

However, when you use a spot color, you can print that color by using only one printing plate at a time. So, if your publication uses only two or three colors, then it makes sense to use spot colors for printing because only two or three printing plates are needed. But if your publication uses four or more colors, then it is advisable to use process colors because then you'll need to have a printing plate for each additional color, which will add to the production cost.

As a result, you might find it necessary to convert a spot color to a process color. This means the spot color is recreated by using the four inks. To do this, select the spot color, open the Color Options dialog box, change the color type to process in the Color Options dialog box, and click OK.

Do it!

A-5: Converting a spot color to process color

Here's how	Here's why
1 Observe the color type icon of the color My red	It is a spot color.
2 Double-click the color **My red**	You'll change the color type of this spot color to process color.
3 From the Type list, select **Process**	
Edit the Name box to read **My process red**	
Click **OK**	The My process red color appears in the Colors palette.
4 Observe the Color type icon of My process red	The color type has changed to process color.
5 Update the publication	

Topic B: Using color libraries

Explanation

PageMaker has a collection of colors called *libraries*. You use these libraries to add colors to the Colors palette. Once you've created colors in a publication, you can save them in your own color library, and then open and use this library in other publications.

Color libraries

Color libraries are color sets organized into specific categories. By default, PageMaker has 20 color libraries, such as Crayon, Greys, and PANTONE. These libraries contain thousands of colors to pick and choose from. You can add colors from any of these libraries to the Colors palette.

When your publication will go to a professional printing press, it is advisable to use PANTONE colors, which is the common color standard used by printers. These colors are designed to conform to the paper coating standards, and each color is numbered, which makes it convenient for printers to reproduce the colors consistently. With that in mind, you'll use a particular library depending on the expected output.

Do it!

B-1:   Selecting a color from a library

Here's how	Here's why
1 In the Colors palette, select **None**	(If necessary.) Use the Pointer tool.
2 Click [⬛]	
3 From the Libraries list, select **Crayon**	The Color Picker dialog box opens displaying the Crayon Library.
4 Select the color **Maroon**	
5 Click **OK**	To close the Color Picker dialog box and return to the Color Options dialog box.
6 Click **OK**	The color Maroon appears in the Colors palette.
7 Update the publication	

Custom color library

Explanation

A custom library can contain any combination of PageMaker's default colors, colors from various libraries, or custom colors created by you. Once it is created, you can use a custom library in any other publication.

To create a Library, choose Utilities, Plug-ins, Create Color Library.

Do it!

B-2: Creating a custom color library

Here's how	Here's why
1 Choose **Utilities**, **Plug-ins**, **Create Color Library...**	To open the Create Color Library dialog box. This will create a library of all the colors in the Colors palette.
In the Library name box, enter **My library**	
Edit the Colors per column box to read **3**	
Click **Save**	To close the Create Color Library dialog box and save the color library.
2 Open the Color Options dialog box	You'll open your color library.
3 From the Libraries list, select **My library**	The Libraries list has various color libraries.
4 Click **Cancel**	To close the color library.
5 Click **Cancel**	To close the Color Options dialog box.

Topic C: Adding colors to objects

Explanation

Objects are added to a publication to add visual appeal. These drawn objects, imported images, and even text can have color applied to them, which will further increase the visual interest of a publication.

Apply colors to objects

When you have to add the same color to multiple objects, you can select all of the objects and add the color to them. You do this by pressing Shift and clicking on each object with the Pointer tool, and then selecting a color from the palette.

Do it!

C-1: Applying color to multiple objects

Here's how	Here's why
1 Move to the second page	
2 Click as shown	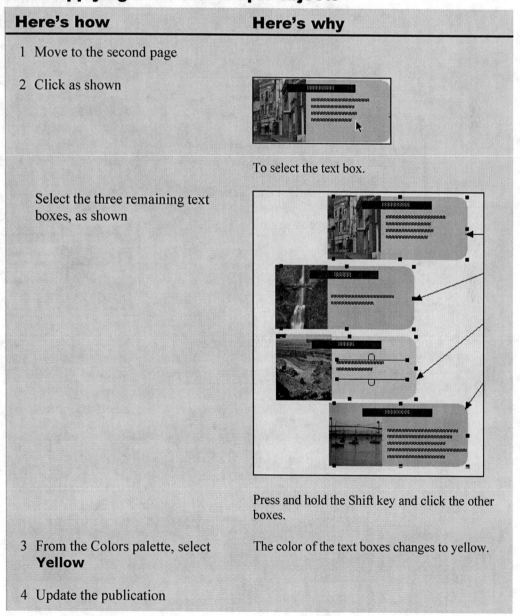
	To select the text box.
Select the three remaining text boxes, as shown	
	Press and hold the Shift key and click the other boxes.
3 From the Colors palette, select **Yellow**	The color of the text boxes changes to yellow.
4 Update the publication	

Apply color to imported objects

Explanation
You can import images, such as photographs or artwork, into your publication. Once the image is on the page, you can add color to only if it is a grayscale TIFF image.

To add color to the image, select the image and use a color fill.

Do it!

C-2: Applying color to an imported object

Here's how	Here's why
1 On page 3, select the map	You'll add color to the black-and-white picture of the map of the USA. You can add colors only to grayscale TIFF images.
2 Right-click the map	A shortcut menu appears.
Choose **Link Info...**	To open the Link Info: Map.tif dialog box.
Under Link Information, observe Kind	The image of the map is a grayscale TIFF image.
Click **Cancel**	To close the dialog box.
3 From the Colors palette, select **My green**	The color of the map changes to green.
4 From the Tint list, select **90%**	To make the color lighter.
5 On page 2, select the picture, as shown	
6 Open the Link Info dialog box	
Under Link Information, observe Kind	This image is an RGB JPEG image.
Click **Cancel**	
7 From the Colors palette, select **My orange**	You are not able to change the color because you can add colors only to grayscale TIFF images.
8 Update and close the publication	

Unit summary: Working with colors

Topic A	In this topic, you learned how to **add** a color to the **Colors palette**. You also learned about the different **color models** and **color types**.
Topic B	In this topic, you learned how to **use** the **color libraries** and **create** your own **library**.
Topic C	In this topic, you learned how to **add** colors to **multiple objects** and **imported objects**.

Independent practice activity

1 Add a process color to the Colors palette that is CMYK **20**, **45**, **60**, and **30**, respectively, and name it **My brown**.

2 Create a 40% tint color based on **My brown** and name it **My tint brown**.

3 Open Practice colors.

4 Save the publication as **My practice colors**.

5 Change the background color of the Cinnamon and Cloves frames to the color **My beige** at **55%** tint, as shown in Exhibit 2-2. (Hint: Click the frame boundary and not the text to select the background frame.)

6 Close the Colors palette.

7 Update and close the publication.

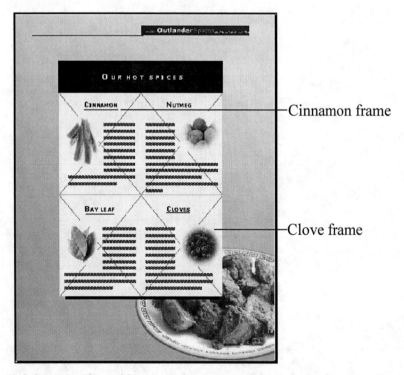

Exhibit 2-2: The publication after step 4 of the Independent Practice Activity

Unit 3
Managing colors

Unit time: 50 minutes

Complete this unit, and you'll know how to:

A Set up and change the preferences of a Color Management System and select image profiles.

B Set and use trapping techniques.

Topic A: Using the Color Management System

Explanation

Printing a color publication with accuracy is difficult because different hardware devices recreate colors in different ways. To retain color accuracy, you need to set up a Color Management System. This helps coordinate colors between devices to reproduce the correct color shade. You can apply this system on imported images or to images you create.

Color Management System

Your monitor, scanner, camera, or printers process colors in different ways. To avoid color changes across devices, you need to set up a Color Management System (CMS). The CMS keeps the color information intact by mapping it through the CIE color model. The *CIE color model* describes colors that are device independent. (CIE stands for Commission Internationale de l'Eclairage, or International Committee on Illumination.)

PageMaker supports two Color Management Systems, Kodak Digital and Apple ColorSync. After you install PageMaker, you can use Kodak Digital but to use Apple ColorSync, you need to install ColorSync control panel device and extension and profiles. The ColorSync system is for Macintosh machines only.

Do it!

A-1:   Discussing a Color Management System

Questions and answers
1 What is a Color Management System (CMS)?
2 Why do you need to set up a CMS?
3 How does a CMS work?
4 What is the CIE color model?
5 What are the CMSs supported by PageMaker?

CMS preferences

Explanation

The CMS preferences adjust the monitor, printer, and image source settings. All color systems have similar preferences. The following table lists the various preference settings in the Color Management System Preferences dialog box, as shown in Exhibit 3-1.

Setting	Function
Color Management	Turns CMS on or off. Turn CMS off if you do not need it. This will save memory and increase the speed of performing tasks in the software.
Monitor Simulates	Simulates composite or separations printers. You can view the output on your monitor depending on the type of printer. Composite printers print the proof of a publication and separations printers print the final output of a publication.
New Items Use	Specifies the color profile to use while importing colors. You can have a device profile for each hardware device in addition to the CMS setting.
Kodak ICC Settings	Specifies the device profiles for your monitor, printer, and any input devices, such as a scanner.

To set CMS preferences:

1 Choose File, Preferences, General to open the Preferences dialog box.

2 Click the CMS setup button to open the Color Management System Preferences dialog box.

3 From the Color Management list, select On to activate the CMS.

4 From the New Items Use list, select Kodak ICC.

5 Change the other settings as per the printer specifications.

6 Click OK to close the dialog box.

7 Click OK to close the Preferences dialog box.

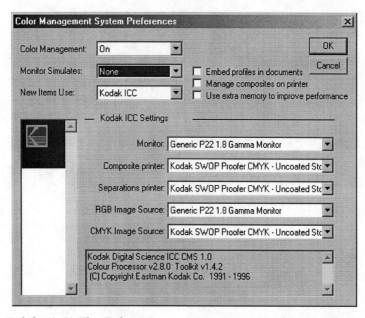

Exhibit 3-1: The Color Management System Preferences dialog box

Do it!

A-2: Setting CMS preferences

Here's how	Here's why
1 Choose **File**, **Preferences**, **General...**	To open the Preferences dialog box. You'll set the CMS preferences and observe the settings.
2 Click **CMS setup**	To open the Color Management System Preferences dialog box.
3 From the Color Management list, select **On**	(If necessary.) To turn CMS on.
4 Display the Monitor Simulates list	You can simulate a Composite or a Separations printer on your monitor.
Click anywhere outside the list	To close the list.
5 From the New Items Use list, select **Kodak ICC**	(On a PC, you have only one option, Kodak ICC.) You'll use this color system to manage colors.
6 Under Kodak ICC Settings, observe the lists	You can specify the device profiles of your monitor, printer, and any source devices, such as a scanner.
7 Click **OK**	To close the Color Management System Preferences dialog box.
8 Click **OK**	To close the Preferences dialog box.

Image profiles

Explanation

As you already know, you can import BMP, WMF, EMF, PICT, TIFF, and EPS file formats into a publication. But to obtain a good quality image when printing, you should use either the TIFF or EPS format.

When you import images without the CMS on, PageMaker will check the imported image for a source profile. An imported image will contain a source profile if it was created in an application with CMS. However, if the image does not contain a source profile, then you can still manage the colors of these graphic images by setting an image profile for them. To set an image profile:

1 Select an image.

2 Choose Element, Image, CMS Source to open the CMS Source Profile dialog box, as shown in Exhibit 3-2.

3 From the This Item Uses list, select Kodak ICC.

4 Click OK to close the dialog box.

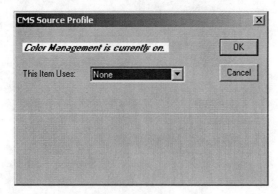

Exhibit 3-2: The CMS Source Profile dialog box

Do it!

A-3: Creating an image profile

Here's how	Here's why
1 Open Image	From the current unit folder.
2 Save the publication as **My image**	In the current unit folder.
Scroll to move the page to the left side of your monitor	
3 Click the chicken dish, as shown	

You'll apply color management to this imported TIFF image.

4 Choose **Element**, **Image**, **CMS Source...**	To open the CMS Source Profile dialog box.
From the This Item Uses list, select **Kodak ICC**	To apply this CMS.
From the Rendering Intent list, select **Image**	To render the image and blend out the colors that are outside the CMYK color range.
Click **OK**	The image of the chicken dish now looks smoother.
5 Update and close the publication	

Topic B: Using trapping techniques

Explanation

When a color publication is printed containing overlapping objects, only the top colors are printed. These overlapping objects could be one shape overlapping another shape or an object on a background. For example, let's say you have a yellow box with a red circle on it. When this document is printed, it is possible that a white edge will appear around the circle. This white edge is called a knockout effect, as shown in Exhibit 3-3. A *knockout* is the area that is left blank for the top color to print. But at times, there will be a gap between the two colors when the top color does not cover the knockout correctly. As a result, you'll be able to see the background of the page as a line between the two colors. To correct this, you use trapping techniques.

Exhibit 3-3: An example of a knockout

Trapping colors

Printing presses use machines with mechanical movements. When a publication is printed with multiple colors or tints, these mechanical movements might cause errors. For example, the printer paper can stretch when moving over color plates, or the paper size can change slightly during the process of print as it soaks up wetting solution and ink. To correct these errors, you can use trapping techniques. You can mark out the point at which two colors join and overprint one of the colors so that it overlaps the other color. This will remove the gap that might appear between the edges of two colors.

Trapping describes the process of creating either a choke or a spread. *Choking* refers to decreasing the color area and is used to minimize the visual impact of traps by trapping a dark foreground object on a light background, as shown in Exhibit 3-4.

Exhibit 3-4: An example of choking

Spreading refers to increasing the color area. A spread is used to minimize the visual impact of traps by trapping a light foreground object on to a dark background, as shown in Exhibit 3-5.

Exhibit 3-5: An example of spreading

You can choke or spread color objects by using any one of the three trapping techniques.

Technique	Function
Mechanical trapping	Used before the introduction of computers in this field. This works by placing a clear material, such as plastic between the printing paper and printing film. When light is passed through the three layers the plastic film diffuses the light and makes the objects appear larger. You can adjust the size by varying the thickness of the plastic.
Object trapping	Used by PageMaker to perform trapping automatically. To trap, apply a line stroke around the color object. The stroke marks the overprinting area. You also need to choose a suitable color for the stroke, which is usually the lighter of the two colors. However, for this you'll have to set printer specifications, such as neutral density of the inks, black limit, line frequency of screens, kind of paper, how loose or tight the press is, how much dot gain, and the position of the paper. Your printer will provide this information to you.
Raster trapping	Used specifically when you have imported graphics in your publication, but requires third party software. The software works by analyzing the entire publication page by page and translating everything to the pixel level. Then the software automatically decides the traps for all the color objects. However, this process is expensive and is used by few printer studios.

Do it!

B-1: Discussing trapping

Questions and answers

1 What is trapping?

2 Why do gaps appear between two adjacent colors?

3 How does trapping work?

4 What is a choke and a spread?

5 What are the trapping techniques?

The Trapping Preferences dialog box

Explanation

In PageMaker, you can use the Trapping Preferences dialog box to set traps in a publication. PageMaker analyzes the publication and registers all the areas where two colors meet. It then creates a trap by using the object trapping technique.

To set the trapping preferences, you open the Trapping Preferences dialog box, as shown in Exhibit 3-6, by choosing File, Preferences, Trapping. The following table lists the options and their functions.

Option	Function
Enable trapping for publication	Turns trapping on or off.
Trap width	Sets the trap width. You can set a trap width from 0.003 picas to 0.0308 picas. You set the higher trap width for black because gaps next to black will stand out.
Trapping thresholds	Sets the trapping conditions. You can set the following options: Step limit specifies the trap limit. The default is 10%. This will create a trap for those colors that vary more than 10%. Centerline threshold specifies when to use the centerline trap. The default is 70%. This will create a trap between colors that are 30% or less apart in neutral density values. Trap text above specifies the condition for trapping text. The default is 23.9 points. This means that text smaller than this value will overprint and text larger will be trapped.
Traps over imported objects	Creates traps for imported objects. This option is usually not used because trapping for imported objects is done best with the raster trapping technique.
Black attributes	Sets the black limit. In printing presses, sometimes the intensity of black is varied. If black is at 80%, then trapping will consider any color having more than 80% black.
Ink setup	Sets the ink neutral density settings. You need not change the settings because the default settings are set by the Graphic Arts Technical Foundation and conform to United States industry standards.

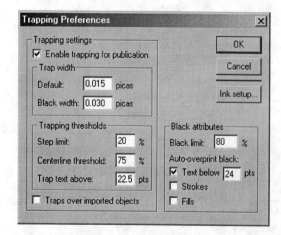

Exhibit 3-6: The Trapping Preferences dialog box

Do it!   **B-2: Using the Trapping Preferences dialog box**

Here's how	Here's why
1 Open Trapping	(From the current unit folder.) You'll set the trapping preferences for this publication.
2 Save the publication as **My trapping**	In the current unit folder.
3 Choose **File**, **Preferences**, **Trapping...**	To open the Trapping Preferences dialog box.
4 Check **Enable trapping for publication**	You can check or clear the option to turn trapping on or off.
5 Under Trap width, in the Default box, enter **0.015**	You can set the trap width from 0.003 to 0.308.
Under Trap width, in the Black width box, enter **0.030**	The Black width is generally double the Default width because gaps next to black will be more apparent.
6 Under Trapping thresholds, in the Step limit box, enter **20**	This will create a trap for those colors that vary more than 20%.
Under Trapping thresholds, in the Centerline threshold box, enter **75**	This will create a trap between colors that are 25% or less apart in neutral density values.
Under Trapping thresholds, in the Trap text above box, enter **22.5**	This means that text smaller than this value will overprint and text larger will be trapped.
7 Under Black attributes, in the Black limit box, enter **80**	Trapping will occur for colors that are more than 80% black.
8 Click **OK**	To close the dialog box.
9 Update and close the publication	

Unit summary: Managing colors

Topic A
In this topic, you examined the **Color Management System (CMS)** and how to set the **CMS preferences**. Next, you learned how to import images correctly by using **image profiles**.

Topic B
In this topic, you examined **trapping** and **trapping techniques** to correct errors in printing. You also learned how to set **trapping preferences** to trap color objects in PageMaker.

Independent practice activity

1 Open Practice image.

2 Save the publication as **My practice image**.

3 Verify that CMS is on.

4 Create image profiles for the four imported pictures. (Hint: Choose Element, Image, CMS Source, and select Kodak ICC.)

5 Update and close the publication.

Unit 4

Working with scripts and plug-ins

Unit time: 50 minutes

Complete this unit, and you'll know how to:

A Use scripts to automate PageMaker processes.

B Use plug-ins to create and perform advanced PageMaker processes.

Topic A: Working with scripts

Explanation

When you create a publication, there are several common tasks that you perform, such as formatting text, images, or graphics. Some of these tasks might be repetitive. For example, you might format a text box and the text in it to a specific attribute. You might then want to apply this formatting style to all the subsequent text boxes you might create. You can do this by automating the task by using scripts. A *script* is a piece of code containing a sequence of commands. All the manual processes in PageMaker can be coded into a script. You can use the default scripts in the Scripts palette to carry out tasks, such as trapping, merging stories, or removing empty frames.

Scripts

Scripts are similar to macros in Word or Excel and batch files in DOS and Windows. Scripts contain a sequence of PageMaker commands. You can store a set of sequences that you need to perform repeatedly. You can then run the script to perform the sequence. For example, you can execute the Remove Empty Frames script to remove all unused frames from a publication.

The Scripts palette

PageMaker provides various categories of default scripts. You can run these scripts from the Scripts palette. The palette lists the scripts, as shown in Exhibit 4-1. You can open the palette by choosing Window, Plug-in Palettes, Show Scripts.

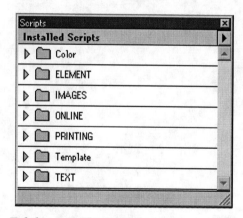

Exhibit 4-1: The Scripts palette

Do it!

A-1:   Examining the Scripts palette

Here's how	Here's why
1 Choose **Window**, **Plug-in Palettes**, **Show Scripts**	To open the Scripts palette.
2 Observe the palette	(As shown in Exhibit 4-1.) It lists various categories of scripts.
3 Click as shown	
	To expand the category and list the subcategories.
4 Click as shown	
	To expand the subcategory and list the scripts.
Select **Remove Empty Frames**	You can apply a script to a publication by double-clicking it.
5 Click as shown	
	To open the Scripts palette menu. You can add, edit, or remove a script.
6 Click outside the palette	To close the Scripts palette menu.

Using scripts

Explanation

You can use the default scripts found in the Scripts palette to perform some common PageMaker tasks. For example, if you want to delete all the empty frames in a publication, you would have to go to each page and search for them. This is a difficult task because an empty frame might be hidden behind another frame or an object. To make your task easier, you can execute the Remove Empty Frames script to perform this task automatically. To use a script:

1   Choose the script category.

2   Choose the subcategory, if necessary.

3   Select a script.

4   Double-click the script to run it.

Do it!

A-2:   Running a script

Here's how	Here's why
1 Open Scripts	(From the current unit folder.) You'll use a script to change the fill and stroke of a box with a single command.
2 Save the publication as **My scripts**	In the current unit folder.
3 On page 3, click as shown	
	The frame behind the text is selected.
4 In the Scripts palette, expand the category **Element**	
5 Double-click **Story Fill And Stroke**	To open the Fill and Stroke dialog box.
6 From the Fill list, select **Solid**	
From the Color list, select **Red**	You'll change the background color of the frame to a shade of red.
From the Tint list, select **60**	To lighten the shade.
7 From the Stroke list, select **2pt**	
From the Color list, select **Blue**	
8 Click **OK**	The background color of the selected frame is now red with a stroke of blue.
9 Close the Scripts palette	
10 Update the publication	

Topic B: Working with plug-ins

Explanation

There are several PageMaker functions that are available in the form of plug-ins. These plug-ins carry out simple commands, such as Bullets and numbering or Change Case for text formatting.

Plug-ins

Plug-ins are options to do specific tasks. These tasks might be formatting or aligning text or converting publications from a previous version to a current one. The following table lists the plug-ins available in PageMaker:

Plug-ins	Description
Add cont'd line	Cuts a text block and adds a small text block telling readers that the story is continued on the next page.
Balance Columns	Resizes all the columns on a page to equal size.
Build Booklet	Prints multiple pages on a large single sheet, which assumes the form of a booklet when folded in a specific manner.
Bullets and numbering	Adds bullets or numbering to selected text.
Change Case	Changes the case of selected text.
Create Color Library	Creates a custom library.
Drop cap	Increases the size of the first letter of a paragraph so that it spans down to cover three to four lines.
EPS Font Scanner	When you print a publication that contains an EPS font, a warning will appear if the font is not installed on your system.
Global Link Options	To specify the location for saving elements used in the publication.
Grid Manager	Sets the parameters for column and gutter dimensions, ruler guide, and baseline data.
Keyline	Creates a stroke around a selected object.
Merge Records	Merges the text and graphics in a data source to PageMaker template.
Publication Converter	Converts a publication created in a previous version of PageMaker to the current version.

Plug-ins	Description
QuickTime Media	Selects and places a frame from a QuickTime movie.
Running Headers & Footers	Used to create Headers and Footers for each story in a publication.
Save For Service Provider	Prepares a publication for a professional printer or service provider by copying all linked image, font, and other files necessary to print your document in one location. It also helps resolve broken links by prompting you to locate missing files.
Show/Hide Toolbar	Displays or hides the toolbar.
Word Counter	Counts the number of words, characters, sentences, and paragraphs in a publication.

Buying and loading other plug-ins

You can also purchase third party plug-ins and use them to improve functions in PageMaker. Some popular plug-ins include PageAlign, PageMover, and PageScaler, which help to design the page layout of a publication.

Do it!

B-1: Using a plug-in

Here's how	Here's why
1 Move to page 1	You'll apply a plug-in to the publication.
2 Choose **Utilities**, **Plug-ins**	To see a list of all the available plug-ins.
3 Choose **Word Counter**	The Word Counter dialog box appears. All the data related to the text in the publication is shown.
4 Click **Close**	
5 Update and close the publication	

Word Counter

Characters:	2236	Text objects:	15
Words:	482	Stories:	15
Sentences:	40		
Paragraphs:	53		Close

Unit summary: Working with scripts and plug-ins

Topic A   In this topic, you learned how to use **scripts** to automate various processes.

Topic B   In this topic, you examined the various **plug-ins** and learned how to use the **Word Counter** plug-in. You learned that the Word Counter **counts** the number of **words**, **characters**, **sentences**, and **paragraphs** in a publication.

Independent practice activity

1 Open Practice scripts.

2 Save the publication as **My practice scripts**.

3 On page 5, select the frame shown in Exhibit 4-2. Then, use the Story Fill And Stroke script to change the fill color to a 70% tint of My peach and the stroke to 2pt Yellow.

4 How many sentences and paragraphs are in this publication? (Hint: Deselect all the frames in the publication.)

5 Close the Scripts palette.

6 Update and close the publication.

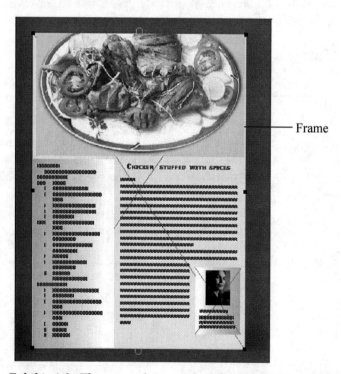

Exhibit 4-2: The page after step 3 of the Independent Practice Activity

Unit 5

Importing and publishing documents

Unit time: 50 minutes

Complete this unit, and you'll know how to:

A Import HTML files.

B Create a PDF document and set the PDF options.

C Create a hyperlink, convert a publication to an HTML document, and use the Layout Adjustment option to adjust page elements.

Topic A: Importing HTML files

Explanation

When you create publications, you might need to import text and graphics from other formats or languages, such as Hypertext Markup Language (HTML). *HTML* is the standard language used to create Web pages and contains a series of tags that define the structure of a Web page. An HTML file has either an .html or .htm extension.

Import HTML files

In PageMaker, you can import an HTML file, including its text, layout, and graphics, by performing the following steps:

1 Open a new publication.

2 Choose File, Place to open the Place dialog box.

3 Select the HTML file and click Open to import the HTML file to the PageMaker publication.

4 Switch to Actual Size view to see the imported contents.

5 Save the publication and close it.

You can also import an HTML file by dragging the HTML file to a PageMaker publication. To do so:

1 Open a new publication.

2 Open the HTML file.

3 Position the PageMaker window and the browser window adjacent to each other.

4 Select the content to be imported and drag it to the publication.

Do it!

A-1: Importing an HTML file

Here's how	Here's why
1 Open a new publication	
2 Choose **File**, **Place...**	To open the Place dialog box.
3 Select **Spices**	From the current unit folder.
4 Click **Open**	To import the contents of Spices.html to the PageMaker publication.
5 Move to the first page	If necessary.
Switch to Actual Size view	
6 Scroll through the page	To view the contents.
7 Save the publication as **My spices**	In the current unit folder.
8 Close the publication	Without saving the publication.

Topic B: Creating PDF documents

Explanation

When you send your publication to a printer or service bureau, you need to send the PageMaker file along with all the embedded fonts and graphics. This can end up being a long list of files, especially if you use two or three fonts in the entire publication and multiple graphic images on each page. You can simplify this process by converting the publication to a Portable Document Format (PDF) document. This file format reproduces the publication in a ready to print state and does not need additional files for fonts and objects.

PDF documents

A PDF document is an ideal method for the electronic distribution of a publication, because it is stored in a compressed state and has a small file size.

Once you've created the PDF file, it can be viewed by anyone who has a copy of Adobe Acrobat Reader. This application is free and available on the PageMaker CD or as a free download at www.adobe.com. This is why PDF is such a popular format and is often used to distribute documents electronically in e-mail or on a Web site.

Do it!

B-1: Understanding PDF documents

Questions and answers
1 What is a PDF document?
2 Why do you use PDF documents?
3 How do you open and read PDF documents?

Create PDF documents

PageMaker uses a separate application called Adobe Distiller to convert publications to PDF documents. To create a PDF file from a publication, you:

1 Choose File, Export, Adobe PDF to open the PDF Options dialog box.
2 Specify the necessary changes.
3 Click Export. The Export PDF As dialog box appears.
4 In the File name box, specify the filename.
5 Click Save. At this point, the Adobe Distiller is creating the PDF file. When it is completed, the PDF file opens in Acrobat Reader.
6 Choose File, Exit to close Acrobat Reader.

Before you can create a PDF file, you need to install Adobe Distiller and a PostScript printer driver on your computer. You can find Adobe Distiller in the PageMaker 7.0 software CD that you have purchased. You need to double-click the setup program and follow the installation procedures. You can also install any PostScript printer driver provided in the CD.

Do it!

B-2:   Creating a PDF document

Here's how	Here's why
1 Open Outlander	(From the current unit folder.) You'll convert this publication into a PDF document.
Save as **My Outlander**	
2 Choose **File**, **Export**, **Adobe PDF...**	To open the PDF Options dialog box.
3 From the PDF Style list, select **[Print]**	You will create a PDF file optimized for printing (file size will be larger), as opposed to one that is optimized for screen (file size is smaller).
4 Click **Export**	(To export the PageMaker publication to a PDF file.) The Export PDF As dialog box appears.
5 Edit the File name box to read **Outlander spices**	
6 Click **Save**	Notice all the progress bars and dialog boxes while the publication is converted to a PDF document. Adobe Distiller is now creating the PDF file.
Observe the screen	The PDF document opens in Acrobat Reader.
Click **Accept**	(If necessary.) If a Software License Agreement window appears, click Accept.
7 Close Acrobat Reader	Choose File, Exit.
8 Close the publication	

Topic C: Creating documents for the Web

Explanation

After designing a publication, you might decide that besides printing it you need to publish a page of it or the whole thing on the Web, which is just one of the ways in which information is exchanged on the Internet. The *Internet* is an interconnection of thousands of computer networks located all over the world.

Any *Web site* you visit on the Internet is a collection of information represented in documents called *Web pages*. These pages are made up of text and graphics. They are not too different from many of the publications you might create, such as a product brochure or an annual report. You can convert these publications into Web pages by exporting the publication to the HTML format.

Adding hyperlinks

All Web pages have links to other documents or pages in a Web site. Adding hyperlinks to text or images creates these links. *Hyperlinks* act as bookmarks and contain the address to the link. You can add a hyperlink by using the Hyperlinks palette.

To add a hyperlink:

1 Open the Hyperlinks palette.
2 From the Hyperlinks palette menu, choose New URL to open the New URL dialog box.
3 Enter the Web address in the URL box and click OK. The URL will appear on the palette.
4 Using the Text tool, select some text. You will apply the URL to this text.
5 On the Hyperlinks palette, click the icon to the left of the URL name to create the link.

Do it!

C-1: Adding hyperlinks to a publication

Here's how	Here's why
1 Open Links	(From the current unit folder.) You'll add a hyperlink in the publication.
2 Save the publication as **My links**	In the current unit folder.
3 Move to page 3	
4 Switch to Actual size view	
Scroll to the lower region of the page	
5 Choose **Window, Show Hyperlinks**	To open the Hyperlinks palette.

6 Click as shown

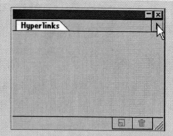

The Hyperlinks palette menu appears.

7 Choose **New URL**   To open the New URL dialog box.

Edit the URL box to read **http://www.OutlanderSpices.com**

Click **OK**   To close the New URL dialog box.

8 At the lower region of page 3   You'll add a hyperlink to link this text with the
   select the text   URL you created.
   www.OutlanderSpices.com

9 Click as shown

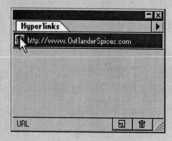

The New Source dialog box appears.

Edit the Name box to read
Outlander Spices

Click **OK**   To close the New Source dialog box.

10 Click ✋   : 735-555-0948 Fax: 735-555-098
                                              Visit us at www.OutlanderSpices.com

A rectangular box appears around the text to
indicate that it is now a hyperlink.

11 Point to the rectangular box   : 735-555-0948 Fax: 735-555-098
                                              Visit us at www.OutlanderSpices.com

The shape of the pointer changes to a hand with
a pointed finger.

12 Update the publication

Layout adjustment

Explanation

When you export a publication, the page size can change, which will throw all the elements in a page out of alignment. You can control this change by using the automatic Layout Adjustment option. To do this, choose File, Preferences, Layout Adjustment to open the Layout Adjustment Preferences dialog box. You can adjust the page elements and ruler guides in the Layout Adjustment Preferences dialog box, as shown in Exhibit 5-1.

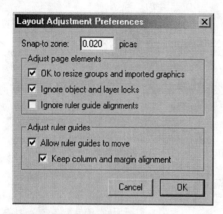

Exhibit 5-1: The Layout Adjustment Preferences dialog box

Do it!

C-2: Using the automatic Layout Adjustment option

Here's how	Here's why
1 Choose **File**, **Preferences**, **Layout Adjustment...**	To open the Layout Adjustment Preferences dialog box.
2 In the Snap-to zone box, enter **0.020**	To specify the area around a page edge and nonprinting guides within which objects are aligned.
3 Check **OK to resize groups and imported graphics**	(As shown in Exhibit 5-1.) The groups and graphics in a publication will be resized proportionately with the resizing of a page.
4 Click **OK**	To apply the changes and close the dialog box. You will not see any visual difference at this point, the changes are apparent when you export a file.

Export to HTML

In PageMaker, you can export a publication to the Internet in the HTML format. To export a publication in the HTML format, you can either convert the entire publication to a single HTML file or save each page as an individual HTML file. You can use the Layout Adjustment option to control the alignment of the elements in the exported HTML file.

To export a publication in the HTML format:

1 Choose File, Export, HTML to open the Export HTML dialog box.

2 Click Edit to modify the HTML settings. You can select the page or pages to convert to HTML and click Done.

3 Click Document to specify the destination folder where the HTML document will be saved.

4 Click Graphics to specify the destination where the graphic files will be saved.

5 Click Options to specify how the graphic files are to be saved and click OK.

6 Click Export HTML to convert the publication.

Do it!

C-3:   Exporting to HTML format

Here's how	Here's why
1 Choose **File**, **Export**, **HTML...**	To open the Export HTML dialog box.
2 In the HTML Document Title box, select **Untitled1**	The Document and Graphics buttons are now available.
3 Click **Edit**	(The Export HTML: Edit Contents dialog box appears.) To edit the contents of the HTML document.
Edit the Document Title box to read **Locations**	
Click **Rem All**	To remove all the pages from the Assigned To Document list to Unassigned list.
From the Unassigned list, select **Page 2**	You'll create an HTML page of this page.
Click **Add**	To move page 2 to the Assigned To Document list.
Click **Done**	To return to the Export HTML dialog box.
4 Click **Options**	To open the Options dialog box.
Under Graphics, under Export as, select **All to GIF**	(If necessary.) All the imported images in the page will be converted to the GIF format.
Click **OK**	

5	Click **Document**	To open the Document Save As dialog box.
	Navigate to the current unit folder	(If necessary.) To save your HTML document in this folder.
	Edit the File name box to read **Locations**	
	Click **OK**	
6	Click **Graphics**	To open the Browse for Folder dialog box.
	Navigate to the current unit folder	To save the GIF files in this location.
	Click **OK**	
7	Click **Export HTML**	An HTML Warning dialog box opens stating that PageMaker boxes, ovals, and polygons are not exported.
	Click **OK**	To continue exporting the HTML.
8	Choose **Start**, **Programs**, **Accessories**, **Windows Explorer**	To locate the HTML document you created.
	Navigate to the current unit folder	You'll see the HTML document you created.
	Double-click **Locations**	The HTML document will open in Internet Explorer.
9	Close Internet Explorer	
10	Close Windows Explorer and return to PageMaker	
11	Update and close the publication	

Unit summary: Importing and publishing documents

Topic A   In this topic, you learned how to import an HTML file to PageMaker.

Topic B   In this topic, you learned about **PDF documents** and their use for the electronic distribution of publications. You also learned how to **export** a **publication** to a **PDF document**.

Topic C   In this topic, you learned how to create **hyperlinks** in a publication and convert it to an **HTML document**. You also learned how to set the **Layout Adjustment Preferences** to compensate for different paper sizes while exporting publications.

Independent practice activity

1 Open a new publication.

2 Save the publication as **My practice locations**.

3 Import the contents from **Practice locations.html** to the publication.

4 Switch page 1 to Actual Size view.

5 Update and close the publication.

6 Open Practice links.

7 Save the publication as **My practice links**.

8 At the lower region of page 3, create a hyperlink to link the text www.OutlanderSpices.com with the Outlander Spices Web site. (Hint: Use the URL for Outlander Spices.)

9 Update the publication.

10 Export the publication to a PDF document optimized for print and named **My practice links**.

11 Close Acrobat Reader.

12 Export page 1 to an HTML document named **Chicken recipe**. (Hint: Choose File, Export, HTML. Remember to change the Export File to Location for both Documents and Graphics.)

13 Preview the HTML page you created in step 12 in Internet Explorer.

14 Close Internet Explorer.

15 Close the Hyperlinks palette.

16 Update and close the publication.

Unit 6
Advanced printing

Unit time: 70 minutes

Complete this unit, and you'll know how to:

A Perform prepress processes by using Image Control and create a PostScript file.

B Create, modify, and use printer styles.

C Understand screen and printer fonts and print color separations.

Topic A: Performing prepress processes

Explanation

Before you send a publication to a printer or service bureau, you need to prepare the publication for print. One such preparation is to control the brightness and contrast of an image to ensure proper reproduction.

Image Control

At times, you will find it necessary to modify an image to increase the print quality. However, in PageMaker, you can modify a two-color or grayscale image by using the Image Control command to adjust only the image's lightness and contrast. The changes occur by increasing or decreasing the number of dots per inch in the image. The more the dots per inch, the darker the image.

The options available in the Image Control dialog box are listed in the following table.

Option	Description
Lightness	Changes the brightness of an image.
Contrast	Creates a color contrast between objects in an image.
Screen patterns	Sets the printing pattern. By default, it is set to dot screen. You can set it to line screen for special effects.
Screen angle	Sets the angle for printing. By default, it is at 45°.
Screen frequency	Sets the number of lines per inch to be printed. The default value depends on the type of printer.

To use Image Control:

1   Select a two-color or grayscale image.
2   Choose Element, Image, Image Control to open the Image Control dialog box.
3   Change the values in the Lightness and Contrast box.
4   Click Apply to observe the changes.
5   Click OK to close the dialog box.

Do it!

A-1:   Using Image Control

Here's how	Here's why
1 Open Prepress	From the current unit folder.
2 Save the publication as **My prepress**	In the current unit folder.
3 Select the map of the USA	(In page 3.) You'll apply Image Control settings to this image.
4 Switch to Actual Size view	To view the image at 100% zoom.
5 Choose **Element**, **Image**, **Image Control...**	To open the Image Control dialog box.
In the Lightness box, enter **−20**	To reduce the lightness of the image.
Edit the Contrast box to read **65**	To increase the contrast of the image.
Click **Apply**	The image is now darker.
6 Observe Screen patterns	Screen patterns:
	These are the two options in which the dots can be printed.
7 Edit the Screen angle box to read **35**	To specify the angle as 35°. This change will not be visible on the screen, but only when the publication is printed.
8 Edit the Screen frequency box to read **15**	This is the number of rows of dots per inch that will be printed. This change will not be visible on the screen, but only when the publication is printed.
9 Click **OK**	To close the dialog box.
10 Update the publication	

PostScript file

Instead of sending a PageMaker file with all the linked images and fonts to a printer or service bureau, you can create a file called a PostScript file. A *PostScript* file encapsulates all the linked images and fonts and contains instructions and formulas on how to print a specific publication correctly.

To create a PostScript file, you'll first need to verify that a PostScript printer driver is installed on your computer. If necessary, you can install one from the PageMaker 7.0 software CD or from the manufacturer of your PostScript printer. After installing a PostScript printer driver, you use PageMaker to create the PostScript file:

1 Choose File, Print to open the Print Document dialog box.

2 From the Printer list, select a PostScript printer driver.

3 Click the Options button to open the Print Options dialog box.

4 Check Write to PostScript file.

5 Click Browse to specify the location where you want to save the file and click Save.

6 Click Save to save the PostScript file for the publication.

Using a PostScript file

After you've created a PostScript file, it can be sent directly to the print shop. The printer then uses an interpreter to read the PostScript file and creates a raster image of each page. A *raster image* is a bitmap image with a finer grid of dots. By sending the file to the printer this way, you end up with a better output than that of a conventional printer.

You can also use a PostScript file to create a PDF file in Adobe Distiller. Before you can do this, though, you'll need to install Adobe Distiller from the PageMaker 7.0 software CD. You double-click the setup program and follow the installation procedures. Then, with Distiller open:

1 Choose File, Open to display the Acrobat Distiller - Open PostScript File dialog box.

2 Locate a PostScript file, select it, and click Open.

3 In the Acrobat Distiller - Specify PDF File Name dialog box, type the name of the PDF file in the File name box and click Save.

Do it!   **A-2:   Creating a PostScript file**

Here's how	Here's why
1 Choose **File**, **Print...**	To open the Print Document dialog box.
2 Verify that the Printer is set to a PostScript printer	If necessary, select a PostScript printer.
3 Click **Options**	To open the Print Options dialog box.
4 Check **Write PostScript to file**	
5 Click **Browse**	
Navigate to the current unit folder	(If necessary.) You'll save the PostScript file in this folder.
Click **Save**	To save the PostScript file.
6 Click **Save**	To create the PostScript file and close the dialog box.

Topic B: Using printer styles

It's fairly common for a company to send their print jobs to more than one print shop. Each printing press might be using a different printer and will have different printer settings. So it becomes necessary to configure the publication's PostScript file for the specific printer you are using.

Printer style

A printer style stores a specific printer's information. For example, you might be using two different printers to print your publications. The settings and configuration for those two printers might be different, so you'll need to create two separate PostScript files. You can do this by having the printer configurations stored in a printer style. You can then use the printer style to create a PostScript file of a publication specific to that printer. To create a printer style:

1 Choose File, Printer Styles, Define to open the Define Printer Styles dialog box.
2 Click New to open the Name Printer Style dialog box.
3 Enter a name for the style.
4 Click OK to create the printer style with the default settings.
5 Click OK to close the dialog box.

B-1: Creating a printer style

Here's how	Here's why
1 Choose **File**, **Printer Styles**, **Define...**	To open the Define Printer Styles dialog box.
2 Click **New**	To open the Name Printer Style dialog box.
3 In the Name box, enter **My style**	
4 Click **OK**	A new style called My style is created with the default printer settings.
5 Click **OK**	To close the Define Printer Styles dialog box.

Modify printer style

Explanation   You can edit a printer style to modify the preferences or settings.

You do this by choosing File, Printer Styles, Define and selecting the style you want to edit.

Do it!   ## B-2: Modifying a printer style

Here's how	Here's why
1 Choose **File, Printer Styles, Define...**	To open the Define Printer Styles dialog box.
2 From the Style list, select **My style**	You'll edit the printer settings for this style.
3 Click **Edit**	The Print Document dialog box appears.
4 Click **Paper**	The Print Paper dialog box appears.
Under Paper, in the Size list, select **Letter**	To change the paper size from A4 to Letter.
Under Paper, check **Page information**	Page information is printed at the bottom of the page.
5 Click **Options**	The Print Options dialog box appears.
From the Data encoding list, select **Send binary image data**	The data will be transmitted in the binary mode.
Click **OK**	A message box appears, stating that the page will not fit on the selected paper size.
Click **Cancel**	To return to Print Options dialog box.
6 Click **Paper**	
From the Tiling list, select **Auto**	Under Fit, you'll notice that the description now reads "4 Tile(s) per publication page. Assembled tiles represent the entire publication page."
Click **OK**	To close the Print Paper dialog box.
7 Click **OK**	To close the Define Printer Styles dialog box.

Using printer styles

Explanation

After you have created or modified the printer styles, you can use them to print a publication or to create a PostScript file of a publication. To create a PostScript file using a printer style:

1   Choose File, Printer Styles, and the style you have created.
2   Click Options.
3   In the Write PostScript to file box, enter the printer style you have created.
4   Click Save.

Do it!

B-3:   Using a printer style

Here's how	Here's why
1 Choose **File**, **Printer Styles**, **My style**	To open the Print Document dialog box and create a PostScript file with your printer style.
2 Click **Options**	
3 Edit the Write PostScript to file box to read **My printer style**	
4 Click **Save**	To create the PostScript file and close the dialog box.
5 Update the publication	

Topic C: Printing proofs

Explanation

Before the final printing, you need to make sure that the proper fonts are available; otherwise, the fonts you see might not be the fonts that are printed. You can also print separate sheets for each color in a publication to check for the correct color intensity. The color proofs are used to confirm the color choices and reproduction of the images.

Fonts

When you create a publication, you have to ensure that printer and screen fonts are installed on your computer. *Printer fonts* are PostScript fonts and are created by mathematical formulas and codes. *Screen fonts* are used to display printer fonts on the screen. You need both types of fonts to ensure that the correct font is printed. Using printer fonts in your publication is the best way to ensure the expected output. However, if you use TrueType fonts, then the PostScript driver will convert the font to a PostScript font. *TrueType fonts* are fonts that are printed exactly as they are visible on the screen. The quality of the output in this case will depend on the quality of the conversion.

Do it!

C-1: Discussing types of fonts

Questions and answers
1 What are the two types of fonts?
2 What are printer fonts?
3 What are screen fonts?

Color separations

Explanation

In PageMaker, you can print the colors in a publication on separate sheets to check the color intensity of the image. These sheets are also called *color proofs*. Proofs are used to verify the color reproduction of an image. To do this:

1 Choose File, Print to open the Print Document dialog box.
2 Click Color to open the Print Color dialog box.
3 Select Separations to display the color list.
4 Select All to Process to convert all colors to CMYK mode.
5 Click OK.
6 Create a PostScript file for the printer.

Do it!

C-2: Printing color separations

Here's how	Here's why
1 Choose **File**, **Print...**	To open the Print Document dialog box.
2 Click **Color**	The Print Color dialog box appears.
3 Select **Separations**	
Observe the indicated area	

	The list and the buttons are now active. The list has all the colors in the Color palette.
4 Click **All to process**	A message box appears, indicating that the conversion might change color effects.
Click **OK**	The list now displays only the CMYK colors.
5 Click **Options**	You'll assign a new name to the PostScript file.
6 Click **Browse**	The Write Postscript to File dialog box appears.
Edit the File name box to read **Separations.ps**	
Click **Save**	
7 Click **Save**	To save the color separations to a PostScript file.
8 Update and close the publication	

Unit summary: Advanced printing

Topic A   In this topic, you learned how to use the **Image Control** option to change the **contrast** and **lightness** of an image. You also learned how to create a **PostScript file** for the printer.

Topic B   In this topic, you learned how to **create**, **modify**, and **edit** a **printer style**.

Topic C   In this topic, you learned about the differences between **printer** and **screen fonts**. You also learned how to print **color separations** to check color intensity.

Independent practice activity

1 Open Practice prepress.

2 Save the publication as **My practice prepress**.

3 Apply Image Control on the image of the map of the USA. (Lightness = **-15**, Contrast = **-60**, and select the diagonal screen pattern.)

4 Create a PostScript file named **Practice prepress** for this publication.

5 Create color separations for this publication and save them as a PostScript file named **My practice separations**.

6 Update and close the publication.

7 Close PageMaker 7.0.

PageMaker 7: Advanced

Course summary

This summary contains information to help you bring the course to a successful conclusion. Using this information, you will be able to:

A Use the summary text to reinforce what you've learned in class.

B Determine the next courses in this series (if any), as well as any other resources that might help you continue to learn about PageMaker 7.0.

Topic A: Course summary

Use the following summary text to reinforce what you've learned in class.

PageMaker 7: Advanced

Unit 1

In this unit, you learned how to use the **story editor** to **check the spelling**, **find** and **replace** text, **remove** extra spaces and returns, and **change text attributes** of a publication. Next, you learned how to **adjust line length**, select a **typeface**, and apply **hyphenation** and **justification** to a publication.

Unit 2

In this unit, you learned how to **add** a **color** to the Colors palette. You also learned about the different **color models** and **color types**. Next, you learned how to use the **color libraries** and **create** your own library. Finally, you learned how to add colors to **multiple objects** and **imported** objects.

Unit 3

In this unit, you examined the **Color Management System** (CMS) and learned how to set the **CMS preferences**. You also learned about **image profiles** to import images correctly. Next, you examined **trapping** and **trapping techniques** to correct errors in printing. You also learned how to set **trapping preferences** to trap color objects in PageMaker.

Unit 4

In this unit, you learned how to use **scripts** to automate various processes. You also examined the various **plug-ins** and learned how to use the **Word Counter** plug-in. You learned that the Word Counter **counts** the number of **words**, **characters**, **sentences**, and **paragraphs** in a publication.

Unit 5

In this unit, you learned how to import an HTML file to PageMaker. Next, you learned about **PDF documents** and their use for the electronic distribution of publications and learned how to **export** a **publication** to a **PDF document**. Then, you learned how to create **hyperlinks** in a publication and convert it to an **HTML document**. You also learned how to set the **Layout Adjustment Preferences** to compensate for different paper sizes while exporting publications.

Unit 6

In this unit, you learned how to use the **Image Control** option to change the **contrast** and **lightness** of an image, and to create a **PostScript file** for the printer. Next, you learned how to create, modify, and edit a **printer style**. Finally, you learned about the differences between **printer** and **screen fonts** and learned how to print **color separations** to check color intensity.

Topic B: Continued learning after class

It is impossible to learn to use any software effectively in a single day. To get the most out of this class, you should begin working with PageMaker 7.0 to perform real tasks as soon as possible. Course Technology also offers resources for continued learning.

Next courses in this series

This is the last course in this series.

Other resources

Course Technology offers additional learning resources for PageMaker 7.0. For more information, visit www.course.com.

PageMaker 7: Advanced

Quick reference

Button	Shortcut keys	Function
		Opens the Document Setup dialog box
	CTRL + O	Displays the Open Publication dialog box
	CTRL + S	Saves the publication
		Opens the Insert Pages dialog box
	CTRL + 1	Changes the view to Actual Size
	ALT + CTRL + E	Opens the Text Wrap dialog box
	CTRL + 0	Changes the view to Fit in Window
	ALT + CTRL + F	Opens the Frame Options dialog box
	CTRL + M	Opens the Paragraph Specifications dialog box
	CTRL + D	Opens the Place dialog box
		Creates oval and circular frames
		Creates rectangular frames
		Crops graphics
		Types, selects, and edits text
		Selects, moves, and resizes objects

Button	Shortcut keys	Function
▤	(SHIFT) + (CTRL) + (L)	Left-aligns the text
▤	(SHIFT) + (CTRL) + (R)	Right-aligns the text
▤	(SHIFT) + (CTRL) + (C)	Centrally aligns the text
▤	(SHIFT) + (CTRL) + (J)	Justifies the text
▤	(SHIFT) + (CTRL) + (F)	Force-justifies the text
▣		Opens the Color Options dialog box

Index